A Woman of God's Journey

HEATHER LYNETTE

WESTBOW
PRESS®
A DIVISION OF THOMAS NELSON
& ZONDERVAN

WestBow Press books may be ordered through booksellers or by contacting:

WestBow Press
A Division of Thomas Nelson & Zondervan
1663 Liberty Drive
Bloomington, IN 47403
www.westbowpress.com
844-714-3454

Unless otherwise noted, scripture taken from the New King James Version®. Copyright © 1982 by Thomas Nelson. Used by permission. All rights reserved.

Scripture marked KJV taken from the King James Version of the Bible.

ISBN: 978-1-6642-4326-2 (sc)
ISBN: 978-1-6642-4327-9 (e)

Library of Congress Control Number: 2021917223

Print information available on the last page.

WestBow Press rev. date: 10/25/2021

One afternoon.

During midday prayer the lord said to me, I need to write down the things he has done in my life.

This is my first book and everything I have been thought and still am going thought is in this book, had not been for God in my life I would not had made it.

If you are believing for a break though while reading keep the faith like I had to do and the same God that heal me, he can and will do the same for you just keep the faith.

I am praying and believing God that he will move in everyone heart, while reading how I lost my mother, my older sister took ill Friday evening and died on the next day Saturday, but by Gods grace my family and I made it thought the hurt and pain.

My book is mostly about faith, healing and the hard times that we all face each day, at times it was hard for me, but you will see the great ways that the lord held onto my hand, and brough me though each time.

When the enemy tried to take me out of this world God always shows up, it will also Encourage my readers, is my prayer.

Thank you.

Chapter 1

My name is Heather Lynette, and this is my story of the journey that God is taking me through.

I was born in the West Indies. I have lived in the United States for most of my life, finished college here also. I was raised in a Christian home with my three sisters. We all loved the Lord. I have a great family.

Our mother loved the Lord with all her heart. We were always in church, but we loved it. I was a Baptist at an early age, but I stopped going to church and started hanging out with my friends, thinking that I was now grown and my parents could no longer tell me when or how often I needed to be in church. For this reason, I backed away from church and God for a while. I was so busy partying and hanging out with my friends that I did not have time for anything else.

I met someone, but he went to his church on Sundays, so I said that must be okay. After a little while, we started dating, which led to marriage.

God blessed us with two beautiful children, a daughter and a son. We loved our children very much.

Our kids grew up in the way of the Lord. We made sure that all four of us were at church every Sunday morning. We still partied over the weekend, but we made sure that we were in church on Sunday mornings, and the kids went into Sunday school classes.

Psalm 34:15: "The eyes of the Lord are upon the righteous, and his ears are open unto there cry."

Chapter 2

My husband and I had a great relationship. We traveled a lot and took the kids on worldwide trips because of the my job with an airline.

We all loved to travel; almost every weekend the four of us would be on a flight going somewhere for a few days. Then, when we returned home, I would work as much as I could. We would also travel home to the West Indies as often as we could to visit our family and friends.

But things started to go wrong between my husband and me. After about ten years, my marriage started to fall apart, which led to us becoming separated.

I decided that it might be better for me to find a place for me and my kids to live. I faced a life struggling as a single parent while holding down a full-time job. It was the hardest thing that I had ever had to do. I moved out along with my two children; things were just not working out between my husband and me. I also did not want our kids to keep on seeing the two of us not getting along. I thought it would be best if we went our separate ways, but we determined to continue to be great parents.

God had blessed me with a great job, and I was able to afford to live on my own with my daughter and son. At this time, I started to party again with my coworkers and friends every weekend, which caused me to lose all interest in church. Plus, I thought I had no time for church because I was so swamped with family responsibilities.

I always made sure that I spent time with my kids on weekends when they were off from school. We would go to dinner, or I would take them on a trip somewhere out of town, sometimes to Disney World for a few days. I wanted to make sure we had fun together so that they weren't too sad that their parents were no longer together.

Our kids did very well in school. I would always try my best to compliment them and help with their homework as much as possible. It was a little hard being a single parent for a while, but God helped me through it all.

One Sunday morning, my daughter, Kayla, came into my bedroom and said, "Mum, my friend invited me to go to church with her and her family. Can I go please?"

After calling her friend's mother and talking to her about the invitation, I told my daughter it would be okay. She could go to church with them, but I wanted her to make sure they brought her right back home after church was over.

Kayla went to church with this family a few more times, and one Sunday morning, she wanted me to go with them. She came and woke me up, saying, "Mum, this church is friendly. Can we all go together with my friend as a family like hers?"

I had come home from partying all night. I told her I didn't want to go as a family because I was too tired to go, but I said it was okay if she wanted to go to church with them. Her brother did not mind not going to church as long as I did not tell him he had to go. His sister loved going to church with her friend on Sunday.

Chapter 3

During this time, I had received a call from my dad. He told me that my mother had not been feeling well and had passed out early that morning. They'd had to rush her to the hospital. We were trying to get ourselves together to fly home to the West Indies right away. My mother was my heart. I was praying that nothing would happen to her.

My mother had suffered a small stroke, but praise God that my kids and I made it home to see her. She had been discharged from the hospital before we arrived. She had started to feel a little better, so we left and returned home with the intention of going back to see her the next week.

When we were about to leave the house for the airport, I told her, "Love you, Mom. We will see you soon. Okay?"

She replied, "You all will see me, but I will not see you because I asked the Lord to take me home. He was going to, but I prayed and asked God to allow me to see my daughter and grandchildren one more time."

I had backslid from serving the Lord, so I did not receive what she was saying. I asked her to please stop saying those things because she was making me worried. She said okay, but she asked me to promise her that I would give my life back to God and stop living the way I was living at the time. I told her I would. I didn't want her to be worried.

My kids and I left and returned home to the States.

A few days after we got back, I was at work when I received a call from my dad telling me that my mother had gone into the bathroom, fallen, and passed out. They'd had to call the ambulance, and she had been rushed to the emergency room. She was in the hospital, and the doctor said she was in a coma. He said they were still working on her and did not know what was wrong at the time.

I started praying and crying out to God, asking him to not take my mom. Then I remembered what she had told me before we left for the airport.

I told my dad we would be coming home the next day.

Chapter 4

That same night, while I was packing to leave, my aunt called and said she was on her way over to my house to talk with me. I asked her to pray for my mom, but she did not reply. She just said, "See you soon."

My phone rang again. Someone else was calling to say that my husband was on his way to my home. I could not understand why he would be coming so late when the kids were already in bed. It was almost ten o'clock.

A little while after my aunt arrived, she and my husband began to hold me and make me sit down. Then my dad called. My sisters were with him. My aunt picked up the phone, and I heard her say, "We are now about to tell her." Then she said to me that my mother had died not long before. That's all I heard—I passed out. When I came to and opened my eyes, I was on the floor with people standing over me.

I started crying. My dad was still on the phone, and I asked him to please go back to the hospital to make sure she had died for real because hospitals make mistakes all the time. Then he said to me that he was sorry, but she had died right in front of him.

I was so brokenhearted. I did not even know how I would be able to go on without my mother.

I could not stand the thought of having to go home and not see my mother alive. Plus, how in God's name was I going to be able to tell my kids that their grandmother had died?

I began feeling sick suddenly. I could hardly stand up alone. My husband had decided we shouldn't wake the kids because it was so late. He said he would take care of the kids the next morning and let them know what had happened.

I spoke to my dad and sisters for a little while on the phone, but it was so difficult. I could not sleep that night at all no matter how much I tried to.

The next morning, my husband and I waited until our kids got up. We took them into the bedroom and told them we all needed to have a little talk. We both began to hug them. My husband said, "Last night your grandmother went to be with the Lord." They both started screaming so loudly. I was falling apart. I did not know what to do or say. Thank God he was holding on to the kids, trying to comfort them.

Later that day, I had to call my workplace and start making plans to travel home. I kept saying to myself, *How am I going to get this done, Lord?*

We went home. I do not even know how we arrived there. I kept asking my dad what we were going to do without her.

I was out of it—we all were. Our mom was the first person in our immediate family who had died, and it hit us hard. After the funeral, we stayed home for a few days.

When arrived back in the States, I began to feel ill. I didn't want to eat or speak to anyone no matter who the person was. I couldn't fall asleep.

I had to go see my doctor; he said I was going through a depression, and grieving was making things worse. The doctor recommended that I take time off from my job. He gave me some medication to help me relax so that I would be able to get some sleep.

Whenever I closed my eyes, I would see my mom's face. I would jump up and start crying all over again. I could not go to work, take care of my children, or take care of myself.

All I was doing was missing my mom so very much. You see, my mother and I lived far apart, but I used to call her for everything. What made it a lot harder for me was that my mum and dad had come to the States and stayed with me on vacation for a few months. She died when they had been back home for only about three weeks. My kids and I had gotten so used to them staying with us.

During their visit, Mom had told me a few times that she didn't feel well, and she wanted to go back home to see her doctor. Never did we imagine what would happen.

Now she was gone. It was hurting badly. All I could do was cry out to God: "Why did you take her?" I was upset at God for a while, or so I thought.

My husband and other family members and friends had to come to my house to help take care of our kids. I could not see myself going on without my mother at my side because I used to call on her for everything. She was so sweet, and she would always say to me, "You need to give your life back to the Lord; he still loves you." My mom told me she was always praying for me to serve God again and live a better life. She wanted me to stop partying so much all the time.

I would say, "Okay. I will get there someday, Mum." Now that she was gone, it hurt me deeply that I had not rededicated my life to God while she was there praying for me all along.

Matthew 3:2: "Repent, for the kingdom of god is at hand."

Chapter 5

Things began to become so difficult for me as a single parent. My husband had decided that, as long as I stayed away from him with his children, he would no longer help me with anything. He was still distraught over the fact that I had left him and moved out with our children.

For me, life began to get harder. Not knowing what else to do, I started crying out to God with all the strength I had, asking him to please forgive me for the mess I had made with my life.

Every day I prayed hard, but it did not seem to me at the time that God was answering my prayers. I began to think that the Lord was so upset with me that he was not even listening to me at all.

I started looking back on my life and seeing how I had turned my back on God when I had known better, and now I was married but separated. I had two children, whom I loved so very much with all my heart. And I did not have much help taking care of them.

I continue praying to ask the Lord for his help; meanwhile, I worked hard, spending long hours at my job. But still, I did a little partying on some weekends.

One day, a friend of mine invited me to go to church with her on the following Sunday. At first, I thought she must be kidding me, but for some reason, I said, "Yes, I will go with you."

I thought I was doing better because I had cut back on so much partying and hanging out.

I had a dirty little mouth, but only when someone got me upset. I never cursed in front of my children, no matter what. I tried hard not to do that. I didn't smoke, and I kept limits on my drinking. But I loved to have fun, or so I thought. I even started spending more time with my kids instead of having them stay with a babysitter for too long.

I went to the church with my friend and my kids. It was a small church, but the service was amicable, so I decided to go again on the following Sunday. Soon we were going every Sunday.

A few Sundays after I started going regularly, my friend introduced me to the church's pastor and his wife. They were very friendly, and they welcomed us into the church. They told me theywould love to have us come again. I agreed and said I enjoyed the service.

The pastor told me that, if I ever wanted to talk about anything, both he and his wife were always available. I said thanks and thought that it was very nice of them to say that.

The next week after the service, I went up to the pastor and told him I would like to speak to him and his wife because I believed that my life was about to fall apart.

When we met, they prayed with us and encouraged me to rededicate my life to the Lord; God had already forgiven me they said.

Thank God for a praying mother! I did not even remember that she had been going to God on my behalf every chance she got, lifting me in prayer that I would turn my life back around and served the Lord again.

The sad thing for me was that my wonderful mother had already gone to be with the Lord in heaven. It was still hurting me that I had wasted so much time being out in the world instead of serving God, knowing that's what my mother had wanted all along.

I rededicated my life to the Lord after much prayer, and I could feel God's loving arms as he welcomed me back. Then I knew that God still loved me and always will.

Thank you, Jesus, for loving me. I loved the Lord then, and I still do right now with all of my heart. I always will continue to love my God, never turning back again.

God's Word says, "For God so loved the world that He gave his only begotten Son, that whosoever believeth in Him should not perish, but have everlasting like" (John 3:16).

Chapter 6

Then it all started. My kids and I moved from where we had been living to start our lives in a new place where we would be living for the Lord.

At that time, I did not know that the enemy would come after me so hard. I thought that this new journey in my life would be smooth and worry free. Well, that's what I thought. That was so wrong.

God's word says in Isaiah 54:4: "Fear not for thou shall not be ashamed, neither be thou confounded, for thou shall not be put to shame for thou shall forget the shame of thy youth and shall not remember the reproach of thy widowhood anymore."

Thank the Lord! I don't need to be ashamed of my past anymore. Amen.

That is when I realized that God is and will always be with my children and me. We started going back to church as a family. A few months later, we joined and became members of that same church.

I started to pray and began reading God's word more. But I began to feel that the more I prayed, read God's word, and attend church, the harder our lives became. Because I didn't have additional income, I was unable to pay my bills on time. Plus, I was still not receiving any help of any kind.

My ex became more upset with me because, when he heard that I had given my life to the Lord and was in church, he began asking the children if I was involved with anyone in the church. He wondered if I had become involved with the pastor or one of the band members. I chose not to pay any attention to his comments.

As a little girl, I always loved to sing and wanted to sing at every opportunity. At church I was allowed to join the praise and worship team. I have a good voice, and the pastor told me they would love to have me with them.

My ex allowed the enemy to put the wrong thoughts in his head.

I was happy singing and praising the Lord with my sisters and brothers in the church, and I refused to let anything that was said get me down. I kept on thanking God and believing he would provide for my family.

I reached a point when I felt that I could not take it anymore. Some days I did not even have food to give to my kids to eat, and I was way too proud to ask the pastor or anyone in my church for help. They all thought everything was great with us.

The pastor always prayed for my kids and my safety knowing that we lived alone.

In Psalm 23:1, we read, "The lord is my shepherd I shall not want."

Chapter 7

One afternoon, the landlord called me and said she would like to speak with me as soon as I had a chance. That same evening after I left work, I went to speak with her. She told me that they had decided to help me make better payment arrangements. To make payments on time, would it help out if I could pay every two weeks?

I told her it would. She said I could pay half at the beginning of the month and the other half in the middle as long as the full payment was in before the first of the following month. They would be willing to work with me until I could get myself back on my feet.

I said thank you to her and went home praising and worshipping God for working things out for us. God always answers prayer when we least expect it. When we give him thanks for the little things, that's when he blesses us with the big things that we pray for. Amen.

I started praying, asking God to send us help. I asked for an opportunity to move into our own place where we would have our privacy. I kept on praying and trusting the Lord for a new home.

After all of that happened, the Holy Spirit told me to call my pastor and set up a meeting, which I did. He agreed to meet with me right away. I explained everything that was going on with me, and how I was trying to make it with my kids. He started to pray and said he would see what he and his wife could do to help us.

Praise the Lord! That very same week, he came over to see us along with his wife and told me that they had found a new place for us to stay where we would have our privacy, plus it was a move-in ready. I was so happy giving all the praise unto our God for working everything out! Hallelujah! Thank you, Jesus.

The great thing about it was that the landlord did not live there.

God's word says in Romans 8:28, "We know that all things work together for good to them that love God; who are called according to his purpose." Amen.

My God made a way for me to move that same weekend with the help of my church family. I was also able to pay all my rent each month along with my bills, and we had food so we could eat a healthy diet. Thank you, Jesus.

Psalm 23:6: "Surely goodness and mercy shall follow me all the days of my life."

Chapter 8

A few weeks after that, God blessed me again while I was still going through some trials.

I started work at six o'clock every morning. I had no car of my own; therefore, I had to take public transportation to and from work most days. I had to leave my home before 4:45 in the morning to make it to work on time.

Early one Monday morning, I began walking down the street, heading to the bus stop. It was wintertime, and it was still dark outside. While I was walking down the block, there was no one around, but suddenly I heard a young man's voice behind me. He said good morning, and right away he started saying how sexy and beautiful I was looking and what he would like to do to me right then and there.

I looked around, but I tried not to look at him. I noticed no one else walking at that time except the guy who had spoken to me. Not even a vehicle was passing. I started calling on the name of Jesus so fast in my spirit. I heard the Holy Spirit say to me, "Keep on walking and don't look back." Meanwhile, the guy started cursing and getting upset because I did not acknowledge him. My spirit said, "Walk a little faster."

Suddenly, a gentleman came out of nowhere and began opening his newspaper stand. He stood only a few feet ahead of me; I did not see where he had come from, but later I realized he was the shopkeeper. I began praising God for sending someone else.

The guy who was stalking me tried to walk around me and make me stop, but I decided to run into the nearby store. My heart was beating so hard and fast. On my way inside, I said good morning very loudly to the gentleman who was still outside setting up his newspapers.

He followed me inside and said, "Good morning. How can I help you?" I was shaking so much that no words would come out of my mouth.

The young man who had been stalking me was standing outside, looking in at me. His eyes were so red. I kept on praying, asking the Lord to please cover me in the blood of Jesus.

The shopkeeper noticed my distress and asked me if I was all right. He asked me if I would like to sit down for a second. I could hardly get the words out of my mouth, but I said, "Yes. Thanks."

After I sat down on a stool that he gave me, I looked up. The stalker was still walking back and forth outside looking through the door at me. The shopkeeper looked up and saw him standing around outside of the door, so he walked over to the door, but the young man started to walk away.

I waited there for a little while until the day brightened a bit and other people began to fill the streets as they headed to work and school. I thanked the shopkeeper and explained what had happened. I also let him know what a blessing it was for him to have come out when he did. He was so happy he had been able to be such a great help. He said he was going to pray that I would make it to work safely. "From now on, young lady, try to see if someone can walk with you, okay?" he said. "Because there are some unstable people in this world. There have been some guys on the streets early looking for people to mess with, so I'm happy I was able to help you just by showing up at my store."

I told him I would try to find someone to walk with, and I thanked him again. I said, "God bless you, and have a great day."

I continue down the street going to work, all the while giving God all the thanks and praise for surrounding me with his grace.

The Bible says, in Psalm 23:4: "Yea, though I walk through the valley of the shadow of death I will fear no evil, for thou art with me thy rod and thy staff they comfort me."

Chapter 9

After that morning, I started shopping for a car, which I did by faith. On my day off from work, I looked around, checking out used vehicles that were for sale.

One afternoon my daughter, Kayla, and I went into a car dealership and started looking at a few cars. As we looked, we asked the Lord to do us a favor because I did not have a lot of money to spend on a car at that moment.

A salesman came up to us and asked if we needed help with anything.

I explained what we were looking for, and he then said, "Okay, ladies follow me please." Then the gentleman, whose name was Mike, showed us a small car. "Let us go inside into my office and work on some numbers," he said.

We followed him into his office after looking at a few more cars. We were in his office for about five hours while he tried to work out something for us. We kept on praying to ourselves, all the while trusting God to work it out. As children of God, we need to step out on faith and trust the Lord to do the rest. Amen.

At one point, he stepped out of the office, and then he returned and told us that he was waiting for his manager to approve a proposal he had come up with. I thanked him.

As he walked out of the office again, we heard a loud noise. When we looked out of the window, we saw one of those big trucks full of brand new cars driving onto the dealer's lot. The truck was carrying about six cars on top of it. Kayla turned around to me and said, "Mum, it would be so great if we could afford one of those new cars instead of a used one."

I said, "Yes, sweetie, that would be great." We both laughed. We turned and looked out of the window at the cars again; we both saw a dark-blue, four-door Chevy Cavalier, and we both said it together, "I love that one." We started to laugh again.

A few minutes later, Mike came back into his office smiling. "Great news, ladies. My boss said you are approved, but why do you want to take a used car when you can get a *new car*? You guys are in luck because we just received a new shipment."

We jumped up out of our chairs and said, "What? Really?"

The salesman said, "Yes, ladies. Follow me outside, and let's look."

While we were walking behind him, all I could do is keep on saying "Thank you, Jesus" over and over in my spirit.

That evening I was approved to purchase the same blue car that we had looked at through the window. Look what God can do if we only keep the faith and trust him. We finished all the paperwork. When the salesman placed the keys into my hands, I lifted them to God in front of Mike, asking the Lord to bless them.

We then thanked him so very much for all of his help. I said, "You were very friendly and helpful to us, and I hope you have a great evening."

He replied, "Thanks, ladies. I wish you both the same. Enjoy your *new car*, and please be safe, okay?"

Kayla and I got into our brand-new car—praise the Lord—and we began to plead the blood of Jesus all over it before I began to drive. The mileage was at zero, and the plastic was still covering all the seats.

I called my son, Jamar, and yelled into the phone telling him we had just brought a new car. We were all so happy! God had done it again.

He will bless you in the middle of your trials as long as you trust in him when you pray. Amen.

All I could say was, "Look at my God!" And we had a praise moment right there in the parking lot.

We had been there for so long that the dealership was already closed, so there was no one else around, only Mike and his boss, who were getting ready to leave.

I started our new car up, and we drove off.

I would like to pause here and encourage anyone who is reading this book. Always remember that the enemy will come after us, as children of God, with all he has. He will threaten us more than he will threaten sinners because he wants to keep us out of the kingdom of God. My sister, my brother, no matter how hard your trials may get, stand firm, keep the faith, continue praying. It is going to be hard at times, but hold on to God's hand. If our God can do it for me and my family, he can also do it for you. There were times when I wanted to give up.

He loves us so much that he will not let the enemy put more on us than he thinks we can handle. Amen.

Your breakthrough is here. Believe it. Declare it every day. And most of all, keep trusting.

God says in his word, "In the same way, faith by itself, if it is not accompanied by ation is dead" (James 2:17).

Keep the faith, beloved. God loves every one of us. Even when we are going through a storm, God will bless us right in the middle of it.

In Proverbs 3:5–6, we read, "Trust in the lord with all thine heart and lean not unto thine own understanding in all thy ways acknowledge him, and he will direct thy paths." Amen, amen, and amen.

Chapter 10

We loved the church we were attending at that time; it was as if everyone belonged to a big family.

The Sunday after I bought our new car, I shared my testimony during the service. I told everyone how God had just blessed my family with a new car. Praise the Lord! It was a blessing to so many people.

One evening during service, the pastor said, "You can't have a testimony without going through the test first."

That always kept me going when I felt like giving up.

Our praise and worship team received invitations to minister at other churches. I loved that; we made it fun working for the Lord.

One day, a spirit of confusion stepped in. All kinds of problems started happening in our church, and many meetings were held in an effort to sort them out. Still, people continued to complain about everything; then, it spread to us.

A husband and wife separated because of rumors. This went on for a while despite all the extra prayers. Things got worse, and we did not know what to do. People started leaving and taking their kids with them. We had to call for an urgent prayer meeting. We prayed so hard, as we had never prayed before.

The head of the church did not know what to, but the good Lord in heaven worked it all out, and everything changed. It was better than it had been before.

Chapter 11

Things had also got a lot worse between my ex and me.

Everything started to go wrong after the September 11 bombings. I lost two of my very good friends. They worked for the airline. One was a captain, and the other was a flight attendant. They were both on the first plane that crashed.

I had spoken to both of them the day before. They had told me they would have lunch with me the next day when they brought the flight back.

I was about to go on my vacation, but I did not feel like traveling at that time. Thank God for that.

It was so hard. I had just turned on the TV when I saw, all of a sudden, an airplane fly into the building. I thought for a second that it was a movie. But then the news commentator announced that it was real. That broke my heart. I started praying and crying out to God at the same time.

My company began laying off employees, but because I had so many years in the company, my position was not affected.

Still, it was very stressful. I was promoted to the position of general manager.

Chapter 12

One afternoon, my son, Jamar, and I went to church for Bible study at our church. I began to feel a sharp pain in my chest on my left side during the service. I began to pray, but suddenly, the pain started to worsen. I told my friend who was sitting across from me, and she called out to the pastor, who then called Jamar.

They stopped the service and began praying for me, but the pain did not stop. Jamar then had to call the ambulance to take me to the emergency room. By the time the paramedics arrived, my left arm was starting to get numb. They rushed me to the hospital right into the emergency room.

After the doctor examined me, he said, "Ms. Lynette, the symptoms you are having suggest that you had a heart attack.

I did not receive that. I started praying to myself, asking God to please spare my life for my children.

I was in the emergency room for a few hours. The doctors were still running tests on me, and I was hooked up to all sorts of machines. Jamar never liked seeing me so sick. The pastor took him home and brought Kayla in to see me.

While I was lying there in that hospital bed, I started thinking that it seemed as if my life kept going from one sad thing to the next all the time. I started asking the Lord, "Why is my life so hard, Lord? I served you with all that I have, and yet, still, it seems like every bad thing keeps on happening to me. Lord, this is so not fair at all. Jesus, please help me not have a heart attack and leave my children while they are still so young. Lord, I need you right now to help me."

I did not hear an answer from the Lord at that time, so the spirit of fear began to set in, which started to cause my heart rate to go up a little more. The doctors came running, and they had to give me something to calm me down.

The doctor admitted me into the hospital that same night. I remained in the hospital for about seven days while the doctors ran all kinds of tests. Early one morning, a doctor came to me and asked, "How are you feeling this morning?"

I told him I was doing better at that moment.

Then the he said, "Great. Glad to hear that. But the good news is that we have not found anything wrong with your heart. Your heart is very healthy; therefore, you did not have a heart attack, but we will run one more test to make sure, and that is a stress test."

I said, "Thank you, Jesus."

The next day, after my stress test, the doctor came into my hospital room and said, "Okay. Now we have found out what the problem is, and yes you are going to make it. You are going to live." He smiled and said, "If you do everything we tell you to do!" I said I would.

He began to explain that my stress level was so high that it had almost given me a heart attack. The other doctor asked me, "Do you know that stress is something that can kill people?"

I replied, "Yes, sir, but I never thought about it like that."

Then one of them asked me what was going on in my life that caused me so much stress. I told them that I had problems with my job, my church, and my husband. Then the doctor said, "Let me stop you right there. I would like you to answer a crucial question. And I would like you to answer me honestly. All right?" I said I would. He said, "Are any of these things worth dying for and leaving your family?" Then, before I could answer, he said, "Think about it before you answer me, please."

After a few seconds, I replied to the two doctors who were standing next to the bed, "No. Not one of them is worth that."

He then smiled broadly and said, "That is the answer we are listening for. From now on, make sure you put yourself first by taking great care of yourself. We will keep you in the hospital for a day or two more and give you some medication and see how that works before we send you home. But stop worrying. You will be all right. Plus, we will also send in another doctor to check in on you and a therapist to speak to you. So just relax."

After the doctors left the room, Kayla started to cry. All I could do was pray. Sometimes, when something terrible happens, we usually panic first and then pray afterward. Unfortunately, that is what happened to me, but I am so thankful that my God is forgiving. I am also thankful that he is a healing God. Amen.

In Isaiah 53:5, we read, "He was wounded for our transgressions, he was bruised for our iniquities, the chastisement of our peace was upon him, and by his stripes we are healed."

Chapter 13

While I was still in the hospital, the same thing the doctor had just asked me not to do started happening to me again. My mind started going: *What is happening to my kids? Did they eat? Who is driving my car? Is he or she taking good care of it? I wonder what's happening at my job. I hope those kids are not letting anyone into the house. What if their father tries to take them while I am in the hospital?*

At that moment, the door opened, and in came my pastor and his wife and my children, all of them with smiles on their faces, looking happy. I then heard a small little voice say to me., "You have to stop worrying and trust Me. I will never leave you."

The pastor and his wife were taking care of my children. They had all just had dinner together.

The pastor had parked my car at our home the same night I had to be rushed to the hospital; it was safe.

I had to ask the Lord Jesus to forgive me again because then I realized that my worrying was for nothing. The same God who was taking such great care of my children is capable of taking care of me—and every problem I was having.

God said in his word, Isaiah 43:5: "Fear not for I am with thee."

Chapter 14

After the doctor discharged me from the hospital, while driving down the street on my way to an appointment, I noticed that, when I looked into the review mirror, I could hardly see the traffic around me. My vision had been a little blurry lately, and I could tell that it seemed to be getting worse each time I drove my car.

I told my doctor, and he sent me to see an eye doctor the next day. When I saw the doctor, she explained that it was normal for that to happen. It was a small side effect, but it would soon go away. I told her that, when I was in church, I could hardly see the screen. It was also hard to read my Bible at times.

After the exam, I was given glasses for reading, and I was told that my vision would clear up soon; I should not to worry about it.

I wore the glasses for a few weeks. I never liked the thought of wearing glasses. I always prayed asking God, "Please don't ever let me have to wear glasses." Yet here I was. But every chance I got, I would pray and ask the Lord to please heal my eyes so that I could take those glasses off and be able to see better than ever without them.

One Sunday morning during service, I looked up at the screen. My glasses were in my hand, and I was about to put them on, but—thank you, Jesus—when I looked up, I noticed that I could see. Then the Holy Spirit said to me, "Put the glasses down. You no longer need to wear them from now on."

I almost jumped out of the seat. I looked down at my Bible. Everything was so clear that I started looking around the church and could see everything clearer than ever.

Thank you, Jesus, for answering my prayer again.

That was a few years ago, I have not had to wear my glasses since then because I had heard the Holy Spirit telling me not to put them on again.

Even now I don't wear glasses.

Chapter 15

I went back out to work a few weeks after my sight improved only to find out that my boss was about to do a few layoffs that week. My job was subject to layoffs because this was after 9/11 happened. The airline had lost a lot of money, among other things.

After a lot of praying, I decided to go into my boss's office to speak with him to determine what was going to happen.

He explained that the company would be cutting back on some of the staff in our department, but it would not affect management, so I was in the clear.

I asked him, "What if I want to put in for a transfer?"

He explained that he did not ever want to lose one of his best workers, which was how he thought of me.

I let my boss know some of the things I was going through. I told him about the stress, which was the reason I had gone into the hospital.

My boss said he was very sorry to hear that. He did not know that I had so much going on in my life, but he was pleased to see that I was doing a lot better. Then he told me not to worry. He was going to get some more information and get right back to me.

He asked me where I would like to transfer to. I said I was not sure yet. He said that, when I let him know, he would approve it for me. But my boss wanted me to think about it hard before I made any decisions. I told him I would get right back to him.

After praying about it for a few days and speaking with my children and my pastor, I could feel in my heart that it would be a good time for me to move to a new city or state with my children and start over. New beginnings were what I was praying for.

The following week I went back into my boss's office and put in for my transfer to work in another state. He said that would be fine, and he was going to approve it for me right away, but he wanted me to know how much it was hurting him to do it.

I said, "Thank you so much. I know that you are the best boss ever."

I now had ample opportunities for new beginnings for myself and my kids. We were all so excited.

Chapter 16

I knew it would be hard for my children to leave their friends behind, but they looked forward to a fresh start in a new place. Kayla gave me a hard time for a while, but I explained to her a few times what was going on with us, and she understood everything.

Another reason I thought it would be a great idea to move away was that, for some reason, my ex seemed to know everything I did, even how many people I had in my car. I'd had enough of that.

Kayla and I took a few days off and went down to our new town to find a house for us to rent. That way, everything would be in place once we arrived. A short time later, we moved out of the city to begin our new lives, with God going before us, surrounding us with his protection and love.

I had prayed and asked God to help us find a great church where we could grow and have a better relationship with our Heavenly Father.

We moved into a very nice townhouse with so much more room. We all had our own space, and we loved it. There was no one to bother us at all. It was our very own private place. We could yell and shout and didn't have to worry about disturbing anyone above or below us.

The first week that we were there, the Lord showed us a great church not far from where we lived, and he told me this was where we were going to be. It was a megachurch.

That following Sunday, when we arrived at the church, we found it to be so beautiful. When we walked inside and were seated, and I began to look around, I noticed that I used to love watching this bishop on Television Broadcast Network (TBN) every Sunday evening. I almost jumped out of my seat when I saw that we were in his church. I thought to myself,

Look how great God is! This is a powerful man of God. I was looking forward to attending services at this church.

Two months later, we began taking classes to become members of that great church we had grown to love so much.

My job was a little further from home than my last one had been, but that was all right with me because I had my car, which God had blessed me with.

In Romans 8:28, God's Word says, "All things work together for the good of them that love God, to them who are called according to his purpose."

Chapter 17

A few weeks later we all became members of that church. Kayla joined the praise and worship team, and I joined the choir. We began to grow, and we started to learn so much about God's word. I dedicate my life all over to our Lord Jesus Christ again.

I loved the Lord with all my heart. I always say I don't know where I would be without the Lord Jesus in my life, and I was so happy that God had answered my prayer and place us somewhere where we could grow more and get to know him better. Thank you, Jesus.

Things were beginning to feel so much better in our lives. I found myself praying and fasting more. I could feel a difference when I prayed. I also received the gift of speaking in tongues and being baptized in the Holy Ghost.

We all were so happy, starting over in a new place with God on our side.

Kayla and I were sitting in our living room one afternoon when she said, "Mom, I have been praying hard for you. I don't want you to get upset, but I have been praying to ask God to please send a truly wonderful, handsome man of God into your life. I know you said you don't need any stress in your life. Still, I believe that once God sends him, everything will be great between you both. I would love for you to marry again. Mom, Jamar and I have been talking about it. We have been praying over this for a while now, and it just fell into my spirit to let you know."

It was a new church for us, and I realized we can never know what God can and will do. What if he had brought us all the way there to this church for a reason? It would be best not to be living in a house growing older and all alone. My daughter said she asked the Lord that I would not be left alone if she were to get married and move out.

I almost cried when she told me this. I had no idea that my children had been praying for me like that at all. I thought that was so sweet of my kids.

She went on to say, "You have worked so hard for us and have been through so very much. That is why we think that you deserve a good Christian man in your life." Then she said, "We love you, Mom. Please don't be upset."

I replied, "No, I am not upset, sweetie. It blesses my heart to know that you guys are thinking about me in that way. I love you both very much, and if it's God's will that there is someone special in our church, then I pray that God will send him to me, because I am not looking for anyone. I will agree with you all in prayer. I would love to be happy with someone, but I really would not like to get hurt again.

Chapter 18

The following year, on Mother's Day weekend, I was on my way into the mall to purchase a new outfit to wear to church on that Sunday morning because the choir had to minister.

Jamar was with me, and we were sitting at a stop sign waiting to make a right turn into the store parking lot when I heard this thunderous bang. Then realized my car had started moving by itself, heading across the street toward a tree that was ahead of us.

I looked to my left, and I panicked when I noticed all the traffic heading right for Jamar and me. All I could do is say, "Jesus!" I slammed both feet down on the brake pedal, and my car finally came to a complete stop about half an inch from the tree. When I looked back into the rearview mirror, I saw another car pinned onto the back of my car.

I began to feel the worst pain I had ever felt in life, plus I had hit the left side of my head on the metal part of the seat belt, and I had the worse headache ever, all at the same time.

Jamar stepped out of the car as I started yelling for him, asking him if he was all right. He came around to the driver's window and asked, "Mum, are you okay?"

I told him no. I was in a lot of pain. My lower back felt as if someone had poured hot water on it; it was hurting so bad.

A few minutes later, a police car and a fire truck arrived, and I could hear Jamar yelling at someone, but I could not turn around to see who it was. At that same time, I listened to the police asking me if I was okay. I explained to them how much pain I was having, and then another policeman asked the young lady who had come up to my window also why she had driven into my vehicle. "Do you mean to tell me you did not see this car in front of you?" The police officer asked.

The young lady replied, "Yes, officer, I saw her, but my cell phone rang, and when I went to pick it up, it fell on the floor. I meant to hit the brakes hard, but I hit the gas pedal instead by accident." She turned and looked at me and said, "I am so sorry ma'am."

Chapter 19

The young lady's mother had been in the car with her. Instead of coming to find out if my son and I were all right, she got out of the car and started yelling at her daughter: "Girl, wait until your father sees what you have done to this new car! He only just brought it for your birthday! Have you lost your mind? You just crashed a new car the first time you drove it! What is the matter with you!"

I heard the police officer asking her mother, "Wait—is that what you are worried about? What if she had killed these people—or you and herself?"

Then she replied, "Well … sorry. But her father only gave her this car today because it is a birthday gift, and we were going shopping in the mall. I always tell her she doesn't need to keep her phone in her hands all the time. She had no right to be driving with it." Then she walked over to my car and apologized. Then she yelled at her daughter again and told her to come to our car and apologize.

The young girl yelled back at her saying, "I did that already, Mom."

All one of the police officers could say to the others was, "This is too much—for a grown woman to be worried about a car when her daughter could have killed this lady and her son!"

Chapter 20

My head and my back were hurting me so much that I could not even move. The paramedics had to work carefully and with difficulty to safely get me out of the car.

They rushed me to the hospital. Thank God Jamar was okay.

I was in the emergency room for a few hours, but the doctors had me on some pain medication, so I was a little out of it.

After a while, the doctor came to me and said, "Ms. Lynette, you have a serious disk injury in the lower lumbar area of your back. Plus you banged up your head pretty seriously, which will cause you to have headaches for some time. Still, not to worry. With medications and rest, we will have you back on your feet in no time. Okay?"

I replied, "Yes, sir."

As the days went by, my back got a lot worse. I noticed that I could hardly stand up by myself. Sitting was uncomfortable, and getting up was painful. A few days after the accident, the doctor came into the room and said to me, "We have a little bad news. In order for you to walk again on your own, we will have to do surgery on your lower back. But we will get back to you with the details."

I did not receive that. I just asked God to have his way in my life and heal me.

I called my dad and told him what was going on. He, along with a few other family members, advised me that I would be taking a considerable risk going through with back surgery because not everyone has positive results. He told me not to worry. He would put my name down on the prayer list at his church. He would have the prayer warriors lift me and my circumstances to God in prayer. He also told me, "Please keep the faith. You need to pray and believe that God will heal you."

I decided to hold off on the back surgery.

Chapter 21

I was trying so hard not to fall apart. All I could do is say to myself, *Lord Jesus, not again. Please help me!*

After I was discharged from the hospital and was pending surgery, I noticed I could not place any weight on my left leg. I even fell down a few times because of it, but the doctors said that was because the disk was now leaning on the sciatic nerve in my left leg,

All I could do was to keep crying out to God, asking him to help me because I did not know what was going to happen to me. I was taking so much pain medication already. Plus, my right leg was also beginning to get weak.

In the next few months, I could hardly walk by myself. I was given a walker to help me get around. I had to go to doctor appointments at least twice a week and sometimes more.

I went through a little depression. I felt lonely and heartbroken. But, thank God, no matter how sad I felt and how hard the enemy tried to get me down, I had to keep on fighting, telling myself that was the only way I was going to make it through all the hard days and nights.

I could not take a bath by myself at all or get dressed. Thank the Lord for sending one of my very best friends over to help me and the kids. She came to our home most days after she finished work to help me get dressed and take my meds. She did anything we needed. If my kids had to go out, she would stay right there with me in case I needed anything.

My kids loved my friend. Kayla says always, "Mom, had not been for her here helping us, I do not know what would have happened." The great thing about it was that we never had to ask for her help; she came out of the goodness of her heart. That's what a true friend does. Amen.

The Lord blessed me with two of the most beautiful children who stood by my side all the while. They took turns helping me get back on my feet and convincing me not to give up on life. I was too young for that. My kids would tell me, "Keep the faith and stand firm, Mum. God is with you, and so are we."

Isaiah 53:5: "He was wounded for our transgressions, He was bruised for our iniquities, the chastisement of our peace was upon Him, and by his strips we are healed."

Thank you, Jesus! It was over one year before I could walk by myself again, but with God's help, and the help of family members and, friends, I finally got back up. Amen.

My dad would call and pray and encourage me all the time. He would say, "You don't need any back surgery, just pray with faith and believe God will heal you. He can do it!" And that's what I kept on doing. My dad was a really big help to me.

I went back to the hospital, and the doctors ran some more tests. One of them finally said to me, "For some reason, we don't see anything wrong with your back. I am happy to say that you don't need surgery. We don't know how this happened, but you should be okay with a few more treatments and other medications."

Thank you, Jesus! God did it again.

I would like to pause here and encourage anyone who is going through any illness at this time. Just believe in God. Keep the faith when you pray because, if God can heal me, he will do the same for you. The Holy Spirit told me to write this book and tell my readers about everything that he has brought me through and is still bringing me though. I keep asking him to be such a blessing.

God has done so much for me and my family. I don't know where I would be without him. So many times bad things have happened to me. The devil has tried to mess with my health, but our God can take care of us no matter what. Just call on him, and he will answer. There have been times in my life when I thought, *That's it!* But all I said was, "Jesus!" And he was there. His Word says he will never leave us. Amen.

Chapter 22

The doctors sent me to physical therapy about three times a week. I started feeling a lot better, and I began to walk again on my own without using the walker. The pain in my back started to dissipate, thanks be to God. The doctors had told me that physical therapy would be a great help, and it was. I began to walk a little at a time, and praise the great God in heaven, all of this happened without me having to undergo surgery. Praise the Lord!

After being at home for so many weeks, unable to go to church, I was so excited when I felt well enough to go. One Sunday morning, I wanted to go out to church. At that time, I was using a cane to help me get around; the doctors had told me I no longer should use the walker.

Kayla helped me get ready. It was still a little difficult to do a lot of things on my own.

While I waited for her to finish getting herself dressed, I thought to myself, *Maybe you should go wait in the car until she comes*. So I did. Without thinking, I took up the car keys and went outside by myself and got into the car.

I didn't even realize what had just happened until Kayla came out and said, "Thank you, Jesus, for healing my mother. Mum, look at you! You walked out to the car alone. You don't even have your cane. You forgot it and left it in the house. God brought you outside and put you into the vehicle."

When she said that, I jumped and started looking around. I began to call out to the Lord. We both sat in the car, praising God for what had happened.

Chapter 23

For over one year I had not been able to walk alone, take a bath by myself, or dress myself. I had been on so many pain medications simultaneously. It was a tough thing for me to go through. I spent so many days just lying in bed crying. I had always been an active person, and I was still young. At times the enemy would make me think that my life was over.

Thank you, Jesus! It was only a season I was going through.

Psalm 23:4: "Yea, though I walk through the valley of the shadow of death, I will fear no evil, for thou art with me, thy rod and thy staff they comfort me."

Now I can genuinely say that, if God had not been with me, I don't know where I would be today. That is why I have got to praise him every chance I get because, you see, my God has never failed me yet. I thank the Lord for every mountain he has brought me over and every valley he has brought me through.

"I know that my redeemer lives" (Job 19:25).

Thank God for giving me another great testimony. Hallelujah! And I pray that my experiences will be a blessing to others. I want to let everyone know that our God can do anything but fail if we just believe. Amen.

The word of God says in 2 Chronicles 7:14: "If my people who are call by My name would humble themselves seek my face prayer then, I will here from heaven and heal they land."

In the name of Jesus, let me encourage you to speak to your saturation. God said he gave us power and authority to speak to any mountain in his name by faith. My moving prayer is what kept me going each day.

The devil kept trying to get me down. When I was home alone, the enemy would come and say to me, "You will never walk again." But thanks are unto my God who was right there to stop me from listening or giving into temptation or depression.

God word says, in Deuteronomy 31:6: "He would never leave us or forsake us." Amen.

My sisters and brothers in Christ, call on Jesus, and keep the faith. He will answer. Prayer works every time.

I love the scripture James 5:16: "The prayers of the righteous avails much."

Thank you, Jesus, my God. Let us take a few minutes and give him praise right now.

Do you love him? Then tell him.

Do you know him? Call on him.

He is waiting. He wants you to ask him to come into your heart. You must mean it. When you say it, with his arms open wide, he will welcome you.

Call on Jesus right now. He loves you.

Jesus is our Healer, Provider, our Way Maker, Savior Father, Redeemer. He is our everything.

I encourage you to call him, call on him—Jesus. Jesus. Jesus, we love you, Lord. Can't live without you.

God is listening. Worship him. Amen.

He loves a worshiper.

John 4:24 says, "God is a spirit, and there that worship him must worship him in spirit and truth."

Chapter 24

Read your Bible and pray every day. You will see how much your life changes; you can't live without spending time with God.

I was sitting on my bed one afternoon. I asked the Lord to please give me something to do with my hands while I was still at home and had not yet gone back to work.

God answered and told me what to do. He told me to make a bag. I asked him, "Lord, show me how!" He did, and I followed his instructions. I made my very first over-the-shoulder handbag. I was so excited. When my kids saw it, they told me they loved it. They told their friends, and to my surprise, they liked my bag too!

Before I knew it, I was receiving orders for more bags. At that time of the year, it was beginning to get cold outside, and the Holy Spirit gave me another great idea. I began making hats and scarf sets to match my bags.

I had never done anything like this before. God was working through me. Each time I started to make an item, I would hold it up to God and pray on it, asking for his guidance, and each time my item came out better than the one before.

I began to receive so many orders! One afternoon, Jamar came to me and said, "Mum, you need to have someone build you a website. And you need to order some business cards." The Lord gave Jamar a name for my business also.

One day, the Holy Spirit came to me through prayer and told me that I needed to apply for a business license. I said, "Yes, Lord." That same week, Kayla and I went downtown. We walked into the government office, did the paperwork, and with God's favor before me, I walked out of that office the very same day with my license in my hands, even after I had been told it could take a few weeks to receive. God once again poured out his divine favor upon me. I am now a legal business owner.

I had a website built and a Facebook page. Everything else was in place for the start of my new business.

I began to receive so many orders that I needed someone else to help me because orders started to get backed up.

All the thanks and praise belong to our Lord and savior, Jesus Christ, Amen. In Philippians 4:13, we read, "I know I can do all things through Christ Jesus who strengthens me."

The enemy kept on coming after me! But I started going through spiritual warfare.

Chapter 25

Early one Friday morning, I had a lot of things to do. I decided to drive Kayla to work. That way, I would be able to start my day early.

I had a doctor's appointment at around nine. A few hours after leaving my doctor's office, I started to feel sick. I did not have any pain, just a sick feeling. I was a little dizzy and felt as if I was going to pass out. I pulled the car over and tried drinking some water, which did not help me at all. I began saying to myself, *Do not panic.* I cried out to God, asking him to please help me because I didn't know what was happening to me. I started to rebuke, in the name of Jesus, whatever was trying to happen. "I need your help, Lord!"

I still tried to do a few more things, but I started to feel worse so had to stop. In the afternoon, it was time to pick Kayla up from her job. I do not even know how I got the car got to her workplace, but I made it there.

My eyesight was getting cloudy. 'Thank you, Lord" was all I could say.

When she came out of her office, before she even got into the car, she yelled, "Mum, what's wrong? Why do you look like that?"

I had to ask her to come around and drive. When we got home, I started doing my home remedies, but they did not work. I had drunk two full bottles of cold medication over the previous days, plus I could hear myself breathing hard. My daughter said, "Mom, you need to see a doctor."

I told her, "It's just a bad cold. I don't need to run to the doctor's office for every little thing, sweetie."

A few hours later, I began throwing up, and then I noticed that my vomit was green. By that time, I could not even stand up I was feeling so sick. My entire body was hurting.

This continued for two days. Finally, I agreed to go to the urgent care around the corner from where we lived to see the doctor. Kayla rushed me there.

As soon as the nurse saw me, she ushered me inside into a room. The doctor quickly came to me and started to examine me. After a few minutes, he said, "I have two kinds of news, bad and good. Which one would you guys like first?"

We both said the good one first, and the doctor replied, "The good news is that you are going to make it. And the bad news is that you have pneumonia."

We both said together with loud voices, "What?"

He then replied, "We need to get you started on some medication right away and get you set up on the machines." He then took Kayla over to his desk where they looked at his computer.

Chapter 26

I started feeling as if I was going to pass out. The nurse was standing next to me, holding my hand, telling me not to worry. "Ms. Lynette, everything is going to be all right. It's like the doctor told you—your daughter got you here just in time. If you had waited another three hours, you would have died. So try to relax. You're in excellent hands. We are going to take the best care of you." I thanked her.

I was beginning to feel frightened, but just then the doctor and Kayla came back over to the bed. I noticed that it looked as if she was trying not to cry. I looked up and asked, "Can you please be honest with me and let me know what is going on?"

He then said to me, "I was showing your daughter that one of your lungs is already full up to the top, and the other one is more than half full."

Then Kayla said, "Excuse me, sir, but my mother was not sick at all. How could this happen?"

He replied, "When your mother was leaving her doctor's office, someone walking ahead of her must have had it. Your mother could have touched the same doorknob and then touched her face. The infection could have gone through her nostrils right down into her lungs."

All I could say at that same time was, "Dear Lord Jesus, help me please."

Since then, I have washed my hands every chance I get. Even before the coronavirus pandemic.

After the doctor walked away, I began to pray with all the little strength I had. A few hours later, the doctor called an ambulance to take me to the hospital emergency room. I was admitted into the hospital right away.

The enemy had tried once again to take me out of this earth, but God's word says, "I can do all things through Christ Jesus" (Philippians 4:13).

And I know that, I am more than a conqueror (Romans 8:37).

I began to declare with the little breath I had by saying, "This too shall pass."

Because God's Word says, "By God's strips I am healed in Jesus name" (Isaiah 53:5).

Chapter 27

I was in the emergency room waiting to be admitted into the hospital and trying not to worry. But, God! I was hurting so much. I looked at Kayla, who was sitting watching me, and I could tell by the look on her beautiful face that she was trying not to fall apart on my behalf, but I also knew that she was praying through her tears.

Jamar was away at college; therefore, that made it even harder on her because she had to call him and the rest of the family. But I knew that God would give her the strength she needed because his word says that God will never leave us or forsake us (Deuteronomy 31:6).

I remained in the hospital for the next two weeks, trusting and believing my Heavenly Father to bring me once again through.

In Romans 8:26, we read, "Likewise, the spirit also helpeth our infirmities; for we know not what we should pray for as we ought, but the spirit itself maketh intercession for us with groanings which cannot be uttered."

I was released from the hospital a few weeks later. Thank you, Jesus.

My family members were so scared that I was not going to make it, but after I came home, they told me that my name had been placed on every prayer list by everyone we knew! Prayers had been going up to God for me from all over the world. I know my God is able.

The situation had been a lot harder on my sisters. After I began to feel better they told me that someone we all knew had passed away from pneumonia a few days before I was diagnosed with it. To God be the glory. This is one of the reasons I always praise God and thank him for everything in my life, especially my children and family.

Every morning when I wake up, the first thing I do is to give thanks for yet another day because we never know what will happen throughout that day

There is no distance in prayer. Thank you, Lord, for that.

When I was in the hospital, I began to feel a little better. One day, a lady came into the room and asked if I had health insurance that was accepted by that hospital. I gave her my card, but my insurance was not accepted there.

The lady said, "Don't worry about the bill right now. Make sure you get better and take care of yourself." She wished me all the best. In the meantime, there were forms that needed to be filled out for me. "Your daughter can fill out this paperwork when she visits," the lady said. "And once the information is approved, our office will give you a discount and will set up a payment plan to help with the bill." As the lady was leaving, she turned around, looked at me, and said, "Or maybe—you never know—God may fix it for you."

Praise God! Thank you, Jesus. Amen. All the glory belongs to you, oh Lord, my God. I had to praise him because, once again, something tried to knock me off my feet, but my God always keeps me safe. I am so grateful to our true living God. I always pray and ask him to please help me live a full life that is pleasing unto him. I want to be there for my kids, grandkids, even great-grandchildren!

Chapter 28

When Kayla came in to see me later that evening, I asked her to please fill out the paperwork so I could give it back to the lady the next day.

When it was finally time for me to go home, I was given a lot of medication, but I still had to be on a little bed rest. It was so great to be out of the hospital.

I woke up the next morning feeling great. But I didn't know that, before the end of that same day, I would be so sick that I would be in the hospital again fighting for my life. But I have learned from all the things I have been through that we should always live our lives the best way we can, doing the will of God.

I always have taught my kids, since they were little, that, when they wake up in the morning, the first thing they should do is give God thanks for getting them up. I taught them to place their entire day in his hands. Also, when they go to bed, they should give him thanks again for bringing them through the day and allowing them to go back to bed because so many things could have gone wrong in that one day.

A few weeks later, I was back to myself, and I was also able to return to church. One day, I received the hospital bill. I opened it and placed it on the bed next to me where I was sitting. I looked at the amount. It looked like a phone number, There were so many numbers. The bill amount was $44,360. I placed my hand on the bill and prayed to ask God to take care of it in the name of Jesus. I then put the envelope on my dresser.

I began to feel a lot better. When I went back to my doctor for a follow-up visit, I received a clean bill of health. All the thanks and praise belong to God.

The following week, as I got into my car to go to choir rehearsal, the Holy Spirit told me to check the mailbox before I left, so I did. There were about six envelopes. When I got back into my car, I placed them on the seat and started going through them one by one. I started to open several that looked like bills, but my spirit said, "Maybe you need to open this one." I thought, *Well, this one looks like a bill, and I do not feel like dealing with right now.* See? Sometimes we don't listen. My spirit again told me to open it; therefore, I did.

I opened it and started reading: "Dear Ms. Lynette. First, we would like to thank you for choosing our hospital. We would like you to know that, after going over all of your information, we have decided to cancel your hospital bill of $44,360; therefore, your balance due now is $0."

The letter went on to say that, if at any time I should require medical care, I should remember that the staff at that hospital would be happy to take good care of me again.

I started jumping up and down in the seat yelling, "Thank you, Jesus!" I called Kayla, but I couldn't say any other words but "Thank you, Jesus!"

She kept saying, "Mummy, what is happening?" And she was laughing. But when I explained to her how the Lord had just blessed us in overflow, we both started shouting and praising God together over the phone.

Our God is awesome. He not only healed me; he then canceled the entire hospital bill. Halleluiah!

There is nothing too hard for my God. Amen.

In Ephesians 6:12, we read, "For we wrestle not against flesh and blood, but against principalities against powers, against the rulers of the darkness of this world, against spiritual wickedness in high places."

Chapter 29

Thank you, Jesus, for another new testimony. Amen.

That evening, after Kayla and I had finished worshiping, I went on to the church. I shared my testimony with everyone. My words were a great blessing to many people who were expecting God to do something great in their lives and who were waiting for answers from the Lord for their breakthroughs.

One lady said to me, "Thank you so very much for sharing that with us." She needed to receive something from the Lord. She has been going through a little depression. She had been waiting for God to answer her prayers. Still, after hearing what God had done for me, she knew that he could do the same for her. Also, she told me that my story had encouraged her to keep holding on to her faith. I will keep her in my prayers as well. Very soon, she will be able to share her breakthrough with everyone. She was very nice, always helping others. I knew that she was a real child of God, and he would always be with her.

That's why I believe that we should always try to help each other. You never know what another person might be going through at any moment. There were times in my life when I wished someone would ask me if I was all right or ask me to pray with me and my family. Just because a person looks okay does not mean all is well. At times, even a hug is all that is needed at the end of a hard day.

In Psalm 34:3, we read, "O magnify the Lord with me and let us exalt His name together."

In Psalm 91:3–4, we read, "He shall deliver you from the snare of the fowler, and the noisome pestilence. He shall cover you with his feathers, and under his wings shalt thou trust; his truth shall be thy shield and buckler."

And, in Psalm 23:6, we read, "Goodness and mercy will follow me all the days of my life; i will dwell in the house of the Lord forever."

Chapter 30

One Saturday afternoon, I called home to check in on my dad. He told us he had not been feeling well, so he had gone to see his doctor the day before.

A few months before that, his heart had often started racing for no reason, and doctors had put him on medication. The doctor had told him that he would need to have a pacemaker put into his chest, and the doctor told him it needed to be done right away.

My dad became a little concerned because he had never been in the hospital in all his life, which was a big deal. We prayed over the phone with him. He sounded great; he was not having any pain or anything. He told me that sometimes getting up caused a little dizziness, but that was it.

I hung up and called Jamar, who had moved away to go to college. I told him to keep his grandfather in his prayers because the two of them had a great relationship with each other.

We told my dad that we would call him back the next day, Sunday, and check in on him. The next afternoon, when we came in from church, I said I would call Dad after I got a little rest from the busy week I'd had. I lay across my bed, and I fell asleep.

Our landline phone rang and woke me up. It was my younger sister. She could hardly speak. When I asked her what was wrong, she replied, "Dad's gone!"

I said, "Well, where did he go now?"

Then she tried to explain. She said, "He just died! His body is still on the kitchen floor!"

I began to scream, and Kayla came running into my bedroom. I could not believe it at all; we had just spoken with him a few hours ago.

My sister had called the ambulance. It came quickly, while we were still on the phone, but our dad had already passed. Just like that, Dad was gone.

At times we ask God why bad things have to happen, but not always do we receive an answer.

When I called Jamar, he took the news hard. Later, someone from the college called me and said my son had stopped eating and was finding it difficult to study. It was a lot for him to deal with. "But God knows best" was all we could say.

After Kayla and I came back home from the funeral, we drove down to Jamar's college and spent a couple of days with him. He was living far away from home, and he was taking his grandfather's death hard. It was not easy for him to be all alone during a family emergency such as this.

We all knew that my father had gone to be with the Lord; therefore, we were not worried that it had happened so very suddenly.

The Bible says, in 2 Corinthians 5:8, "To be absent from the body and to be present with the Lord."

Isaiah 53:4 tells us, "Surely he hath borne our griefs; and carried our sorrows."

Chapter 31

When Kayla and I arrived back home, it was hard for a while dealing with the loss of my father.

I began to work on my business again. God blessed me, and I was able to open a store. Things were going great for a while, but after my birthday, the Lord told us to move.

I was going to help my daughter with some new music she was working on. I closed my store, packed up, and we left by faith, looking forward to new beginnings.

God had an assignment for Kayla, which she started to work on after we arrived in our new home. After about two years, the people she was working on the project began trying to take advantage of her; they did not want to pay what they had agreed. Things began to get so bad that it fell into my spirit that she should resign because God had better things in store for her.

We decided to move back to our previous home and get started on my business once more. I was praying about moving when the Lord told us to move to another state. At first, I did not know why I did not want to go since it sounded boring. My spirit said we had to move there, which we did, asking the Holy Spirit to guide us along the way, especially since we did not know anyone who lived there or had any family members who lived there.

After about six to eight months there, we came home from shopping one afternoon. I was so tired that I lay across the bed to relax for a little while. I heard an order in my spirit to place my hand on the side of my right breast, which I did not do at first, thinking it was the enemy messing with my mind. Then I heard that little still small voice telling me I needed to do it. I thought to myself, *All right, Lord.*

I placed my hand on my breast. Then I jumped and started yelling for Kayla at the top of my voice. I asked her to put her hand there. Still, she kept saying, "No, Mummy, please don't even think about something like that. It's not funny, Mum!"

I told her not to cry. I was trying to stay strong myself, so she felt my breast. Then we were both shocked. There was a large lump in my breast, almost the size of a golf ball. I kept saying, "Jesus, no! Help me please! What is this, Lord Jesus?"

Kayla called my doctor and explained what we had discovered. He told her to take me to his office right away. That same day, my doctor told me he did not like what he found. He sent me immediately to a different doctor for a few tests. He told me to return to his office the next day.

I was so scared, but I kept on praying. We were expected at the other doctor's office. That doctor did a biopsy right away to make sure it was what they thought it was before saying anything to me.

The next day, I went back to see my doctor for the results. That was when my doctor said the diagnosis was breast cancer. My life had turned completely around. I did not know if I should start yelling or crying. I did not know what to do.

In our lives, we sometimes do things a little backward. We worry first and then pray when it should be the other way around. Thank God that he is a forgiving God, and he always understands what we are going through.

I had to start treatments right away because of the size of the cancer.

The word of God says, in Hebrews 13:5 that he will never leave us or forsake us. Amen.

Chapter 32

My doctor sent me to a hospital that specialized in the treatment of cancer; he told me that he knew most of the specialists there.

The oncologist started me on chemotherapy treatments right away. I had to be on strong medication because of the size of the mass. In fact, the doctors were trying to figure out how it grew to be so large and still didn't make me feel sick.

A few days after the chemo treatment, I began to feel sick. The doctors said they would have to lower the amount of medication because the first dose was too intense for my body.

I then had to see a surgeon. He told us about all the doctors that who were going to be working with me. He also said that they would need to meet with my family members and me to explain what to expect and when to anticipate what would happen in the weeks and months ahead.

The only family member I had with me was Kayla, who was not doing so well at all with what was going on. Jamar was still away at college. All my other family members lived abroad.

The doctors agreed to have the consultation with just Kayla and me.

Kayla and I prayed all night, asking God for strength to go through this part of my life, but most of all, we prayed to ask God for complete healing.

We arrived at the hospital, and I was so scared. "But, God, you said you are my healer."

The head surgeon came into the room along with two other doctors. We all introduced ourselves, and the head surgeon began to explain to us that ours would be a long journey, but we should not worry because they would be right there with us through it all. They then asked us if breast cancer ran in my family. I replied that, as far as I knew, it did not. I did not remember anyone talking about it.

One of the other doctors said that everything was going to work out. We shouldn't worry because we were going to be in excellent hands. Theirs was one of the most prominent cancer hospitals in the country.

The head surgeon told me that the chemo they would give me would be strong because they had to make the lump smaller as soon as possible before he could even think about getting me ready for surgery.

I jumped and said, "Surgery?"

The doctor told me not to worry, but yes, once they got the lump down to the correct size, I would need to have an operation because there was one lump on the side and another smaller one front. Because they could not cut the breast in half, they would have to remove the entire breast. I needed a total mastectomy.

I almost passed out.

Kayla could not even speak when I looked at her. In my spirit, I was crying out to God asking him, "Why me?"

The doctor went on to explain that I would have to undergo about twelve weeks of chemo, after which I would go back to see him.

I'd had so much pain and heartache already in life, and now I had to deal with breast cancer. I could not believe that I had to endure such a difficult medical condition. I felt like giving up, but I kept thinking about my children. They were grown, but still I asked the Lord to please help me to be around for them, to see them get married and have families of their own.

I started to question God about everything.

After we left the hospital, I could hardly walk or speak. I kept thinking about everything the doctors had just told me and how life had been turned around so much and not even in the right way.

I had to fight so hard, and my family members were helping me not to get deeply depressed. It felt as if the whole world was now on my shoulders, and I was sinking.

Kayla had to tell her brother, which was one of the hardest things she'd ever had to do, she later told me.

The doctor had to perform a small surgery on my neck before the once-a-week treatments started. After the first few days, I began to feel sick again. I was constantly throwing up, I had a temperature, my head was dizzy, and I was in so much pain. We had to call my oncologist. The office staff member told Kayla to take me to the nearest hospital while she kept trying to reach the doctor.

It was almost midnight, so Kayla helped me into the car and drove to the nearest hospital emergency room, which was not far from us. The sickness started to get worse as she drove.

After I was in the emergency room for a few hours, I was so happy that the pain had stopped—for the time being. The doctors had me on so many machines and pain medication. My doctor finally called and told them to transfer me to the cancer hospital where she worked and where I was already receiving treatment.

I was transferred by ambulance to the cancer hospital the following day in the afternoon. I was there over the weekend. My doctor came on Monday morning and said the medication was too strong for my body; that was why I was feeling sick, but she would stop the meds for the time being. I was in the hospital for about two weeks that time. I began to feel a lot better, and my doctor discharged me from the hospital.

We went back to see the doctor a few days after I was discharged. She said she would have to lower the medication a little, but they were still trying to see how fast they could reduce the size of the lump.

The good news was that it was beginning to get a lot smaller, but they wanted to keep on trying to get it down a little more. The smaller it was, the better it would be for the outcome of the operation.

A few weeks went by. I was still horribly sick at times. Then, suddenly, one day after a treatment, I almost passed out again and started feeling sick. Kayla and I began to pray, repeating God's word back to him: "Lord, you said in your Word that you would never leave us or forsake us."

"He was wounded for our transgressions he was bruised for our iniquities; the chastisement of our peace was upon him, and with his strips we are healed" (Isaiah 53:5).

"Lord Jesus, I need you right now, God." That was all I could say because the medication kept on causing me to feel so sick.

Chapter 33

Another doctor came in and said they were going to stop the meds for a day and let my body rest, but in the meantime, I needed a blood transfusion right away. My blood count had gone down considerably, which was causing me a lot of dizziness and headaches. I had no idea what was happening. We had to spend the rest of the day in the hospital for the procedure.

All of this was happening on the weekend before Thanksgiving. "In all things give thanks" (1 Thessalonians 5:18).

I was fighting so hard to give God thanks. Through it all, I was still there even though the devil was trying to make me say, "What if this is what takes me out?"

Thanks to God, it does not matter what the enemy throws at us. Our God can bring us through as long as we trust and believe in him to do so. Amen.

One of my favorite Psalms says, "Yea, though I walk through the valley of the shadow of death, I will fear no evil; for thou art with me, thy rod and staff comfort me" (Psalm 23:4).

All I could do was pray; I knew he would answer.

The doctor came after a little while to check on me and see how my body was taking the blood treatment. I felt a lot better, so I was soon discharged from the hospital with some medication for dizziness.

That was the first Thanksgiving that we could not celebrate in the usual way. I could not eat anything, did not like the smell of most foods, could not even stand the sight of food. I was very hungry, but even water would not stay down in my stomach.

The chemo treatments were not agreeing with me in so many ways. Doctors told me that happens to some people, but there were surprised that I was getting *all* the side effects. They gave me medication, but at that point, it was not working.

It was such a terrible feeling; I didn't even know what to do with myself.

After the holidays, we had to go back to the hospital. The doctors were going to try to start the chemo treatments again to see how my body would react to it this time. God bless my beautiful daughter. She helped me get to all my doctor appointments, plus she was working a full-time job. Thank the good Lord in heaven that she was the boss. The owner of the business understood and gave her a little time to take care of me. At times I would be feeling so sick that I needed help with everything.

So, the doctors set up the machines and got the treatments started again. Each treatment took an hour. After a few weeks, again I started to feel sick with fever, headaches, and throwing up. Everything I tried to eat or drink came right back up.

Kayla had to call my doctor and explain what was happening to me. She was told to take me into the hospital right away. This time all the doctors came in to see me. It was a nice hospital, and I do believe that God blessed me with the best doctors. My doctor said they were thinking that they should stop the treatments and get ready for surgery because my body could not handle the treatments.

The good thing, at least, was that the lump had gotten much smaller. It was not where she would like it to be, but a little better is always a good thing.

The surgeon, whose name was Doctor Dan, said he would call and see what date the operating room would be available, and he would get right back to me.

They all were very lovely doctors, which helped me a lot to go through this. They gave other medications to me that would help. I had the surgery on February 14 (of all days!). Thank God for bringing me through it safely and being in the operating room overseeing it all.

A week after surgery, I noticed that I could not raise my hands up to my face. This meant that I could not feed myself. My hands had gotten weak. Several of my fingers went straight and would not bend at all. My doctor said that it was a side effect of the chemo treatments, but everything should get better after the surgery. That did not happen at all. The nurse had to feed me. It was so bad that the hospital had to discharge me with a nurse and home help.

Like Andrae Crouch's song tells us, "Through it all, I've learned to trust in Jesus."

Chapter 34

A few weeks later, I had to start radiation treatments, which happend every day for a few weeks.

It was difficult going to and from the hospital every day, but I had to pray and ask God to give me the strength I needed to get through this part also, and after much prayer on my part, he did it.

Some days were a lot harder than others. After the treatments, I did not feel so good at all, but the doctors told me that would soon pass.

One day, after I had almost finished the treatments, Kayla and I were about to leave when really strong dizziness overcame me. I could not even stand up by myself. Thank the Lord we were still at the hospital when this started happening. Kayla called out for a nurse to come to me. She immediately sent for the doctors, who came rushing to see what was going on with me.

After running a few tests, they admitted me. The radiation had burned my skin. Again, the treatments were too strong for my body. Still, the doctors said I did not need that much radiation because they had been able to get all of the cancer out during the surgery. Praise God! But they thought just a little radiation was not a bad idea.

My blood sugar went up way too high, along with everything else. I had to be in the hospital for three weeks.

After the doctors ran three CT scans and two MRIs, they still could not determine what was causing the dizziness.

One of the specialists came to the room early one morning and said they believed that I had had a slight stroke. The first CT scan showed a blood clot behind of one of my ears. A second test showed that the blood was running down, which was not good at all.

I asked my daughter to call or text the contacts on her cell phone and mine and ask for urgent prayers. We started praying ourselves right after the doctor walked out of the room.

The next day, my doctor came in early like he always did and said he wanted me to have one more MRI to make sure there were no signs of a stroke. The technician knew me and joked around about being there again. I was terrified about going in that machine, so they always tried to cheer me up.

In two days, two of my doctors came into my room and said they did not even know where to begin or how to even explain what was going on. Therefore, another doctor would be coming to check in on me, and he would try to explain the situation. They told me not to worry, however.

Later that afternoon, my doctor said, "Okay. We have never seen anything like this before. Still, when we checked your results, we noticed that there was nothing there at all. It looks like there was never any blood there ever. I did not know how to explain all of this to you." He went on to say, "I even called in other doctors to look at all your results. They cannot believe or understand what happened because it was there before and now it is gone!"

My daughter and I knew what had happened! God had answered our prayers. As we were listening to what the doctors had to say, we were worshipping in our spirits giving thanks to our Heavenly Father for being in the room with us and answering all the prayers that went and are still going up for me.

Thank you, Jesus. I know my God always answers prayers. Amen. Amen. Amen.

When the prayers go up, the healing come down. Thank you, Lord! My God is able.

Kayla and I went right into a praise break in that hospital room. Our God had done it again! Thank you Jesus! I love you, Lord. You are a great God.

You see, most of the people that my daughter had texted and called were pastors and prayer warriors. I am a prayer warrior. When we all get to praying, mountains have got to move.

All those prayers were going up at the same time—Jesus! Jesus! Jesus! Hallelujah! This is what I kept on saying to myself while the doctor was speaking.

In Ephesians 3:20, we read, "Unto him, that can do exceedingly abundantly above all that we ask or think, according to the power that worketh in us."

We know that prayer works every time. Thank you, Jesus, for healing me from the stroke that the doctors thought they saw. Hallelujah! Hallelujah! Thank you, Jesus.

I could not stop *worshiping*.

I was going through a lot, but I knew that God was with me and he was going to bring me through it all in Jesus's name. I know I am carried in his everlasting arms, and he will never let me go no matter what.

Philippians 4:13 assures us: "I can do all things through Christ Who strengtheneth me.

Chapter 35

He is such a wonderful God. Amen. All we need to do is call on him. Even in our time of need, he will answer.

The dizzy feeling did not stop. Early one morning, my doctor came into the room and said they were going to send me to rehabilitation—rehab—for a few weeks. She continued to explain, "The chemo has several side effects. One is that you can't use both of your hands the way you should be able to. Another is that your walking is not as it should be. Therefore, we think it will be in your best interest to go to rehab because you will be able to receive therapy each day, which will help you get your strength back. If we keep you here in the hospital, you will not get the same care." The doctor then asked if that was all right with me.

I did not want to go, but I said, "Yes. It is okay. I know that it will be best for me."

She explained that everyone there had my best interest at heart. They were so sorry to see that I was going through so much, and they would all keep me in prayer.

I explained the rehab benefits to my kids, and they also agreed that it would be the best thing to do.

The doctor told me that a caseworker would come in before I left to explain how it all would work. That way I would know what to expect once I arrived there. "Good luck with everything," she said. She said she would see me again.

The nurse said she would arrange for an ambulance to take me over to rehab, which was about thirty minutes away. They told me that people did not go home before going to rehab; they went straight from the hospital.

The next day, I was told that the doctor would like to speak with Kayla when she came in and before I left. That is not something you want to hear when you are in the hospital. I had to tell myself a joke or two at times to keep me going. My daughter came shortly after.

When Kala came back to my room, two nurses were about to get me ready because transportation was there to take me to rehab. My daughter would be following behind us in her car.

It was hard leaving the hospital when I was not able to help myself. It was also hard to not be going home. I was about to leave my room in a wheelchair because I could hardly stand or walk by myself.

I want to encourage everyone to keep on trusting God. Believe that everything will work out in your favor. Amen.

I did not know what to expect moving forward, but I knew that God would be with me through it all.

"Trust in the Lord with all your heart and lean not unto your understanding. In all your ways acknowledge Him, and he shall direct tour paths" (Proverbs 3:5–6 NKJ)

When you pass through the waters, I will be with you, and through the rivers, they shall not overflow thee. When you walk through the fire, you shall not be burned neither shall the flame kindle upon you" (Isaiah 43:2).

Fear not!

Chapter 36

When we arrived at the rehab building, a staff member greeted us, saying, "Ms. Lynette, your room is ready for you." The room was big, and at first, I thought that everyone was amicable.

Because I often had dizzy spells, the doctors had ordered that I was not to be left on my own, and I had to use a wheelchair.

On my first night there, at around 11:30, I had to use the bathroom, but I had to press the button to summon help. A lady came in, and I asked her if she could please help me to the bathroom. I needed help getting out of the bed, plus I had to use the wheelchair, which was over in the corner. I was in so much pain my stomach was hurting. It was hard not being able to help myself.

Therapy treatments started the next morning; I was scheduled for therapy early in the morning every day. It was going well. My therapist was very friendly. Actually, all of the staff members were friendly. I did not mind getting up early to go to therapy.

During therapy one morning, I heard someone asking for me by name. My therapist pointed me out. Someone from upper management had come to welcome me.

I had to try hard not to fall into a depression. Again, I asked the Holy Spirit, "Why me?" You know, sometimes we forget what God has already done for us and what he has brought us through. Also, if he has done it before, why question him when we should already know that he is God and he can do it again? God brought me through that day.

After I went back to bed, I saw that my cell phone had rung a few times.

After two more weeks in rehab, I started to feel a lot better and was told that I should be discharged by the following week. My kids and I were so excited. I had been away from home for over two months, so I was so happy to be going home.

I had begun feeding myself and learning how to dress myself again. We should never take life for granted because we never know what can happen. We can go from being in the gym so many times a week, rushing around, to a dramatic change in our lives. I am reminded of the old saying: "Once a man twice a child."

I went from being a business owner, working hard each day, to suddenly not even being able to tie my shoelaces. But at the end of the day, always give God thanks that things are not worse than they could have been.

My therapists had taken me out of the wheelchair and started teaching me how to walk again. About three times a day, they would make me walk, and I was able to do a little more each time. At last, praise the Lord, I began to walk a lot better, but with a walker. I could not go far, but I was walking again.

Thank you, Jesus! Praise the Lord. Amen.

We always need to remember to praise our God no matter what we are going through. Hallelujah!

"And my soul shall be joyful in the Lord; it shall rejoice in His salvation" (Psalm 35:9).

Here is part of one of my favorite songs, "Through It All," by Hillsong Worship:

> You are forever in my life
> You see me through the seasons
> Cover me with your hand
> And lead me in your righteousness
> And I look to You
> And I wait on you
> chorus.
> I will sing to You, Lord
> A hymn of love
> For Your faithfulness to me

I love to worship with this song. The words are so beautiful. Amen.
That is what gets me through.

Chapter 37

My sisters and brothers in Christ, trust God. He said in his word that he will never leave us or forsake us. He is with us through it all. It can be hard at times. I know I have been there, but stay strong in Jesus's name.

When I was discharged from rehab, I was so happy to see the outside world. Kayla picked me up; it was so good to be outside!

The next couple of weeks were not easy. Kayla had to help me shower and get dressed. She prepared all the meals for both of us because I had to be aware of the things I ate and drank. Plus, I was still taking lots of medication.

"Mom, we are in this together. You are my mother, and I am not going anywhere. You have got me for life, no matter how rough things may get. God has brought us this far. I don't think he is going to leave us now, so stop worrying. I love you."

I am telling the world that God has blessed me with two great kids, but I don't know what would have happened to me after my son left home to go to college if it had not been for my beautiful daughter Kayla being there with me and going to a college near home. Through all these trials, one after the other, I don't know how this would have all ended. Kayla even put her music on hold to help me.

My daughter is the best daughter any mother could ever ask for. My son is also the best son. He wanted to be there with us, but had to be in school.

One day I was in the doctor's office at one of my many appointments. We were speaking with one of the staff members, and I told him how great Kayla was, helping me.

He suggested that I let my insurance know that she was the person who was taking care of me before they sent over a caregiver. We applied, and after a little while, Kayla was approved and was accepted as my caregiver.

I had been sent home from the hospital after my surgery with a nurse, but Kayla preferred to help me herself. That's when she decided that she had only one mother, and no matter what it took, she was going to take care of me—all by herself if she had to.

"God is my rock and my salvation whome shall I fare" (Psalm 18:2).

Chapter 38

It took months to get back to myself, and I am still not a hundred percent. I'm getting there.

When there discharged me, they gave me a walker to use. I had to close my business for the time being. Everything was left for my daughter to do on her own, which was a lot for her. Things had already started to get out of hand. I had no idea until I woke up and overheard her listening to a voicemail.

She had not wanted me to worry about anything. But after that, we had to talk. She had not wanted to say anything about what was going on at the moment, but after a little while, she broke down and said that she felt so ashamed and so sorry for letting me down when I needed her the most. I held her and explained that I understood, and I was the person who was sorry.

Still, it was out of our hands. Everything happened so suddenly, and God knew this was all going to happen. We would end up using up all that we had, but we should not worry; rather, we should put all things into God's hands and keep trusting him to work it out for us.

I told Kayla, "I have been praying so hard, asking the Lord not to leave you, sweetie, and God always hears and answer our prayers."

Our family and my best friend had helped, but we did not want them to know that things had become so bad. We had to give up our place before it got worse. We ended up staying in an extended-stay hotel that was like an apartment so Kayla would still be able to cook. We had our privacy, plus it came with everything we needed. It even had internet service. The hotel served hot meals seven days a week, so we had meals if Kayla did not want to cook. It was very nice staying there. It was still a little uncomfortable, however, because we did not want anyone to know where we were living for the time being.

One morning at a doctor's appointment, we were chatting with a lady who worked in the office. She asked what area we lived in. When Kayla told her, she said she lived in that area too. She asked what our house number was. She wondered if we were neighbors and didn't even know it. We did not mind giving her the address because she was one of the people we saw and joked around with each time we saw her.

When my daughter explained our circumstance, she was a little surprised, but she told us that maybe she could help us. She told us not worry; information about our situation would remain between us. No one from her office would say anything to anyone. She left us for a few minutes.

When she came back, she brought along someone who could help us. They explained to us that, once a person has been a patient at that hospital, help was available for whatever he or she needed. Kayla and I said, *Thank you, Jesus!* to ourselves.

The lady then took our information and said, "It might take a while, but I will get things started right away."

One day, a good friend of ours, who is a pastor, came to pray for me. She asked us why we were living there. After we told her what had happened, she said she believed that she could help us get into an apartment right away. She had a friend whom she could call and ask for help. But first, we were going to pray.

We asked God to be in the center of our situation, give us the favor of God, and send the right people along who would help us right now. "Lord, we need you. Also, please send the funds to pay for this place in the meantime. Dear Lord, we are trusting you for a right-now blessing, in the beautiful name of our Lord Jesus. Amen."

God blessed us, and we were able to get an apartment in a few days.

My brothers and sisters in Christ, it may seem that my story is long and mostly a little sad, and to me, at times, I thought it was also. Still, the most critical information I would like each person reading this to receive and understand is that God has been right along with me as I have gone through every trial and every illness that the devil has sent me.

The Holy Spirit sometimes allows us to go through things to make us stronger and encourage others who may be going through the same thing.

One day we can all say, "Lord, thank you for your greatness. Thank you that, when I'm weak, you're strong, Jesus. Lord, I know that the devil is scheming, and I know that he desires to keep me from spending time with you. Don't let him win! Please give me a measure of strength so that I might not give into deception, discouragement, or doubt. Help me to honor you in all my ways, Jesus. Thank you, Lord. You are worthy, and you will never leave me."

One day, the Lord said to me, "I did not give you testimonies so you could keep them to yourself."

It fell into my spirit to write down everything that I have been through with God's help in my life. I am praying that many people will be healed and inspired by reading this book.

Psalm 21:7 tells us, "For the king trusted in the Lord, and though the mercy of the highest, he shall not be moved."

Chapter 39

One afternoon, I was sitting doing a little work, when I received a phone call from my son saying that his father had to be rushed to the hospital.

My daughter went to see him, but things were not looking so good for him at that time. We began to lift him in prayer, asking God for healing over his life, and asking that his situation world not worsen. A lot started going on, but we kept on trusting God on his behalf.

A few weeks later, the kids received another phone call saying that my ex-husband had passed away. It was so hard on my kids. The situation was even worse because we were grieving already at the time of his passing. My older sister had died suddenly, which was one of the hardest things we all had to go through.

I received a long-distance call one evening from my nephew. He told us that they'd had to rush his mother to the hospital. We started to pray as hard as we could. In a few hours, I called back to see what was happening. I was told that she was not looking good at all. My sister was not breathing on her own. Well, we kept on praying. She had been placed on machines to help her breathe. The doctors had to put her in the intensive care unit, but she still did not make it through the night.

Twenty-four hours after we received the first call, she passed away. It was a lot to deal with at the time. Everything happened so fast. She died one year, and then my children's father died the following year.

At times we still find ourselves asking the Lord, "What's happening? Why?"

Then, shortly after that, I started going through everything you can think of. Still, as I always say, God will bless you while you are going through the storms of life. We are just going through rather than staying. We are leaning on God's everlasting arm. Can I get an amen? Anybody?

Psalm 23:6 says, "Surely goodness and mercy shall follow me all the days of my life; and I will dwell in the house of the Lord forever."

Another scripture I love is Romans 8:1: "There is therefore now no condemnation to them which are in Christ Jesus, who walk not after the flesh, but after the spirit.

Chapter 40

As we stand firm in the Lord, the devil will be unable to reach us. No matter what he tries to do, our Heavenly Father will always watch over us once we trust and believe in him.

I still am believing God for complete healing. There are a few little things that are hard for me to do all by myself, but I believe that the same God who brought me this far can finish it all. Amen.

I am keeping the faith that it's going to happen soon—very soon. Amen.

As you believe God for healing in your body right now or for anything else, please repeat this verse with me daily: Trust in the Lord with all thine heart; and lean not unto your understanding" (Proverbs 3:5).

God also says, in Isaiah 43:5: "Fear not for I am with you, I will bring thy seed from the east and gather thee from the west."

And he says in Isaiah 43:19: "Behold i will do a new thing; now it shall spring forth; Shall you not know it? I will even make a way in the wilderness and rivers in the desert."

I read these scriptures each day, among others, to remind myself what the word of God says.

Chapter 41

We need to stay in God's Word every day to grow more in him. Our prayer life will get stronger once we read the Bible and pray every day, more than once a day.

I pray that this book has been a blessing to all who read it, and it will encourage you to keep on believing and trusting God to work everything out that's going on in your lives and also the lives of your family members.

God is always with us no matter where we may go. He's there when we invite him into our lives and mean it. He promises never to leave us alone. Amen.

When the Holy Spirit told me to write this, I did not even know how to begin. What made it seem worse for me is that, after I began to write, I had to think back on everything I have been through. I began to feel so sad about what a hard life I have had. But then God reminded me that he has brought me through it all.

I give God all the thanks and praise for allowing me to tell my story all together at one time. He can and will use everything he has to help us. He helped me to write this story to be a massive blessing for more than one person.

If Jesus was mistreated after he never did anyone any harm, then who am I to complain? God has brought me through this journey, and I will continue to be a child of God.

I plea the blood of Jesus over each page and word of this book. I thank you, Lord, for the wisdom that you have given to me so that I was able to finish this.

A few more scriptures fell into my spirit to leave with you:

Psalm 23:6 "Surely goodness and mercy shall follow me all the days of my life, and I will dwell in the house of the lord forever."

Psalm 46:10–11: "Be still, and know that i am GOD, I will be exalted among the heathen, I will be exalted in the earth. The lord of hosts is with us; the God of Jacob is our refuge."

Psalm 27:14: "Wait on the Lord; be of good courage, and He shall strengthen thine heart; wait, I say, on the Lord."

Chapter 42

One night, I got ready for bed. I felt great after I climbed under the covers. But suddenly my heart skipped a beat so hard that it made me cough. I could not get myself together.

When it happened again, I was so scared I started calling out, saying, "Jesus, help me please!" After sitting up in a chair for a little while, I began to feel a little better. I called my daughter, and we started praying. Nothing like this had ever happened to me before at all.

After I got back into bed, my heart started fluttering. I got out of bed again, and Kayla said, "Okay, that's it, Mom."

She called my doctor, and later that night we found out that some of the medication I was taking created heart issues. My doctor told me to stop the medication right away and told Kayla to keep an eye on me during the night. We scheduled a video appointment for early the next morning. All of this was happening during the middle of the coronavirus pandemic.

After the video appointment, my doctor decided to place a heart monitor on me for two days. He wanted to make sure there had been no damage to my heart.

The following week, I saw a cardiologist. They did all kinds of tests, but praise God they did not find anything wrong.

The only thing that happens now sometimes is that, when I get up from sitting, I became a little short of breath. But God kept me through it all, and I know he will continue to support me.

One of the doctors said some people end up in the hospital with this condition, but I was lucky because I didn't have to. I know that luck had nothing to do with it.

I am a child of God. He said that he would never leave me or forsake me (Deuteronomy 31:6). He will be with me until the ends of the earth.

In Isaiah 54:17, we read, "No weapon that formed against me shall prosper, and every tongue that shall rise against thee in judgment thou shalt condemn."

Chapter 43

Early one evening, I was sitting watching television when my stomach began hurting a little; this kept on happening for a few days. Finally, I could not take the pain anymore. I had to call my doctor.

She told me that I needed to come in and see her as soon as I could.

They could not understand what was going on. I had to have some more tests done. When the tests were finished, it was decided that I would need an operation. We had not expected that.

I started feeling sick, and my doctor sent me to the hospital to have some tests to make sure that my body would be ready for surgery. I had to have the surgery done.

Thank God everything went well, and I starting to feel a lot better again. I have seen my doctor recently, and I don't need to see her again unless something happens.

While I was going through these trials, all the staff members seemed to be having a tough time finding my veins. They needed to do some blood work. A few other nurses tried. Finally, the doctor was able to put an IV into my arm.

The doctor told us that I would need to have a CT scan. My arm began to burn badly, and I started yelling. They told me they would put some ice on it, and they would keep an eye on me, but I should be all right.

Thanks to our God that things are not worse. We know that the enemy is always up to something, but my God said he will never leave us or forsake us (Deuteronomy 31:6). Amen.

In Isaiah 45:2, we read, "I will go before thee and make the crooked places straight."

In Psalm 30:2, we read, "O Lord, my God. I cried unto thee, and thou hast healed me."

Another scripture of encouragement is Psalm 1:1: "Blessed is the man that walketh not in the counsel of the ungodly, nor standeth in the way of sinners nor sitteth in the seat of the scornful.

It fell into my spirit to write down the journey God is taking me through. I am praying that it will be a blessing to my readers.

We all go through different kinds of experiences. God allows us to learn from them.

I want to thank my best friend for all her encouragement and prayers with everything that has been going on in my life.

A huge thanks to my daughter Kayla for standing by me.

I felt so many times like giving up. My son, Jamar, always says to me, "Do not worry, Mum. I know you can do anything you put your mind to. Hang in there. God's got you."

No one in my family or anyone else knew that I was writing this book. I wanted it to be a surprise and also a blessing to them.

Most of all, I give my Heavenly Father all the praise for being with me and never leaving me. I would not be here today if it had not been for the love of God. Amen.

Because of the coronavirus that is going around the world right now, we all need to be very careful. I pray in the name of Jesus that everyone will stay safe. Stay at home if you can. Please wear your mask like the government is asking us to do.

Remember, God is a God of order. We should try to listen to warnings for the safety of our family members and loved ones.

My thoughts and prayers are with those of us who have lost love ones. I pray that our Heavenly Father will continue to give us the wisdom we need to get through this. In Jesus's name.

God bless, and may the peace of God be with you!

Printed in the United States
by Baker & Taylor Publisher Services